THE LIT

PA

TIPS

ANDREW LANGLEY

THE LITTLE BOOK OF PASTA TIPS

ANDREW LANGLEY

A.
Absolute Press

irst published in Great Britain in 2010 by
Absolute Press
Scarborough House, 29 James Street West
Bath BA1 2BT, England
Phone 44 (0) 1225 316013 **Fax** 44 (0) 1225 445836
E-mail info@absolutepress.co.uk
Web www.absolutepress.co.uk

A catalogue record of this book is available from the British Library

ISBN 13: 9781906650452

Printed and bound in Malta on behalf of Latitude Press

'In a country called Bengodi there was
a mountain made entirely of grated
parmesan cheese, on which lived people
who did nothing but make macaroni and
ravioli and cook them in chicken broth.
And the more of them you ate,
the more you had. Nearby ran a
rivulet of white wine....'

**Giovanni Boccaccio, Italian writer
(1313–1375)**

1

Starter or main?

Pasta is quintessentially an Italian food (even if it was invented in China). The Italians tend to treat it as an early course in the meal, and so eat moderate quantities. Outsiders regard it as a main course, and have much larger helpings.

2

A pasta dish is a combination of two elements,

which are cooked separately and then combined. There's the pasta itself – the bland, starchy but irreplaceable backbone. And there's the sauce, which adds the taste, the aroma and the excitement. Give each one the same amount of attention.

3

Know your pasta. There are

two basic groups of pasta – fresh and dried.

Fresh pasta is what you make at home (the shop-bought 'fresh' is best avoided). Dried pasta is the factory-produced stuff you buy in packets.

4

Always buy good quality dried pasta – preferably Italian.

Manufacturers in Italy are bound by law to use use durum wheat (*grano duro*) and no other. This hard grain is perfect for making firm, well-textured pasta. In other countries softer wheat is sometimes used, with predictably limp results.

5

How much should you cook?

This, of course, depends on who's eating. A rough guide is that a 500g (1lb) packet of pasta will provide plenty for four hungry folk as a main course. Daintier diners will need less.

6

There are

three essential bits of kit

for cooking pasta. One is a big saucepan, lidded and preferably tall rather than wide, for boiling. Two is a big colander for draining. And three is a wooden spoon, preferably with a long handle, for stirring.

7

Cook pasta in plenty of water.

The ideal amount is ten times the weight of the pasta, which works out at roughly 2–3 litres (5 pints) of water to 250g (8oz) – that's half a packet – of pasta. This allows for the pasta to absorb a fair bit of water, and dilutes the starch which oozes out. Too little water, and the result will be a sticky mess.

8

Boiling pasta requires

just one extra ingredient – salt.

This adds roundness and interest to the pasta, which is bland by itself. Once the water is boiling, put in at least a tablespoon of coarse sea salt per 500g (1lb) of pasta. Resist the urge to add olive oil, which is pointless.

9

When the water is boiling vigorously

– and not before –

add the pasta.

Sounds obvious, but put all the pasta in at once so it cooks evenly. Give it a stir with the spoon straightaway. Then pop the lid on so the heat builds up again as fast as possible (but see overleaf).

10

Timing is vital.

The aim is to catch the pasta *al dente*, or 'biteable'.

It should be firm

and neither crunchy nor flabby.

Once the water is boiling again, remove the lid and start the timer. Set it to the time indicated on the packet, but use your own judgement and test often as the deadline approaches.

11

Unwatched pasta will soon form a Gordian knot.

So stir it frequently but gently

with the spoon while it boils. This will separate the pieces and prevent them from sticking to the bottom of the pan.

12

When the pasta is nearly done,

take out a few ladles full **of the cooking liquid** and pop it in a bowl.

This will be nice and starchy. You can use it to thin down your sauce if it's boiled away too much, or to moisten the mixed dish at the end if you think it's too dry.

13

Once you've decided it's **done, drain the pasta immediately.**

Dithering will quickly lead to overcooking. Pour the contents of the pan carefully into the colander (previously placed in the sink). Count to ten, then tip the drained pasta back into the pan – or into the pan which contains the sauce.

14

Mix the sauce and the pasta straightaway.

The object is to get the sauce clinging to as much of the pasta as possible without delay. Put both into a warm bowl or pan and toss together very thoroughly with a wooden spoon and a fork. If it looks a bit dry, add a ladle or so of the cooking liquid.

15

Get eating at once. Pasta tastes at its best straight from the pan, so serve it up immediately. Make sure everyone is seated and poised with a fork. You will notice that Italians, especially, get stuck in as soon as they are served without hanging about for anyone else.

16

Choose the pasta to suit the sauce

(and vice-versa). There is a dizzying variety to select from – long or short, flat or tubular, round or ribbon-shapped and so on. As a very rough guide, long pasta goes best with the smoother sauces, while the tubes and other funny shapes are suited to chunkier ones.

17

Make your own.

No pasta tastes or feels better than the fresh home-made kind (unless, as Marcella Hazan says, you live in Emilia-Romagna). The process is easy to learn (with a little application) and no more mystical than making bread. And you can adapt it to suit your own taste.

18

Home-made pasta #1: the ingredients.

Could hardly be simpler. You need 300g (10oz) of plain, unbleached flour – preferably proper Italian 'OO' flour – and three large free-range eggs. Other ingredients are very minor and optional, including a pinch of salt.

19

By hand or by machine?

The best pasta is mixed and kneaded by hand. Machines which mix and extrude pasta dough should be avoided. However, machines are useful for rolling out and cutting the dough – though with enough practice you can master these skills too.

20

Hand-made **egg pasta**

is naturally yellow. But you can

produce other colours,

using natural ingredients. The classic is green pasta, made by adding 375g (12oz) of fresh spinach, cooked, drained and chopped. For red, add 3 tablespoons of tomato purée. Black calls for squid ink, though this is frowned on by purists.

21

Have your pasta-making equipment ready before you start.

The only essentials are a nice big wooden board, a fork, a long kitchen knife and a rolling pin. Round biscuit cutters and a wheeled pastry cutter will also be handy, plus a steel pasta machine with parallel rollers and a crank handle.

22

Home-made pasta #2: mixing and kneading.

Put the flour in a bowl, or in a mound on the board. Make a dent in the middle and break in the eggs. Whisk the eggs gently with the fork, then work in the flour until you have a dough. Knead the dough on the floured board.

23

Polish up your kneading technique.

Sensitive hand kneading will always beat a machine. The object is to stretch and oxygenate the dough. Shove the heel of your hand into the dough ball, then push forwards to flatten and stretch. Fold it back on itself and repeat these motions for about 10 minutes.

24

After the kneading,

give your dough a rest

for at least 20 minutes and no more than 3 hours. This allows the gluten in the flour to regain its elasticity. Wrap the dough in cling film to prevent it from drying out.

25

Home-made pasta #3: rolling.

Roll the dough with a pin, using a stretching rather than pressing motion. Turn after each roll to keep it even. If using a machine, cut the dough into 4 pieces and roll each separately. Repeat 6 times, turning the dough each time. Reset the rollers until you have the thickness you want.

26

Rolling is a leisurely process.

Fresh pasta dough needs gentle handling, or it will lose springiness. Lower the rollers only one setting at a time, and keep the dough lightly floured or it may stick in the machine. If the rolling makes the pasta piece too big to handle easily, cut it in half.

27

Allow your rolled dough **time to dry out,** until it becomes slightly harder. This will make it **easier to cut.**

Spread on a clean tea towel for up to 1 hour, turning over halfway through. It is ready to use when it is dry to the touch.

28

Home-made pasta #4: cutting long pasta.

Simplest of all is tagliatelle: just roll up a pasta sheet neatly and slice it into ribbons with a sharp knife. Unroll each ribbon before cooking. For more uniform shapes, use a machine. Most have various settings to give different widths and shapes, including spaghetti and tagliolini.

29

Once cut, **fresh pasta can be dried** (naturally) **and stored.**

Leave it spread out on towels at room temperature for about 24 hours. Then put in a box or some other breathable container (avoid plastic bags, which encourage condensation) and keep in the store cupboard. This should last for several weeks.

30

To make **ravioli and other stuffed pasta parcels,**

ignore tip#27 and use the rolled dough straight away. For ravioli, cut two sheets about 10cm (4 inches) wide. On the first, put blobs of filling (see tip overleaf) equidistant in two parallel lines. Lay the second sheet on top and cut into squares between the blobs with a wheeled cutter.

31

A classic stuffing for ravioli is spinach and ricotta.

Boil 1kg (2lb) of spinach for a few minutes in scant water. Drain, squeeze dry and chop. In a bowl, mix it together with 300g (10oz) of ricotta, two beaten eggs and seasoning. Add chopped mint or grated nutmeg for an extra dimension.

32

Tomatoes are at the heart of many pasta sauces.

Here is an all-purpose tomato base. Saute chopped garlic for 30 seconds, then add a tin of good quality chopped Italian tomatoes, 2 bay leaves, oregano and a big pinch of sugar. Simmer gently for 30 minutes. Make up your own elaborations.

33

The simplest and quickest

of all pasta dishes is *aglio e olio* -

garlic and oil.

For a few seconds only, saute one crushed garlic clove for each person in olive oil. Add cooked drained spaghetti and mix well. If you wish to embellish, add some chopped parsley or chilli flakes.

34

Grate Parmesan cheese on your pasta.

Sounds obvious, but there are qualifiers. Use Parmigiano-Reggiano if possible (the best), and always fresh, never ready-grated. And remember that certain dishes are much better without cheese, notably anything featuring shellfish.

35

Everyone loves

basil pesto with pasta. Making your own is easy.

Whizz up pine nuts, basil leaves and garlic in a food processor, then add olive oil and grated parmesan. Adjust the proportions to your taste – but be generous with the basil. Add to the pasta and toss thoroughly.

36

Make an **authentic *spaghetti alla carbonara.***

Heat olive oil and saute strips of pancetta or bacon, plus chopped garlic and some fresh sage leaves. Add a slosh of white wine. Mix two eggs in a big bowl with grated Parmesan and/or pecorino and some chopped parsley. Stir in cooked spaghetti and the sauce and mix well

37

Pasta with sardines is

one of the great Sicilian pasta dishes.

Saute chopped onion, chopped fennel tops, sultanas and pine nuts in olive oil. After 10 minutes, add chopped anchovies and fennel seeds. Toss with some cooked penne or rigatoni, lay filleted sardines on top and bake for 15 minutes under foil.

38

Farfalle (bowties) go perfectly with peas and pancetta.

For a bag of pasta, saute 100g (4oz) of chopped pancetta in olive oil. Add 200g (8oz) of peas – fresh if possible. After a few minutes, toss with cooked farfalle. Ricotta is an optional extra. Parmesan and black pepper are compulsory.

39

Experiment with your own versions of pesto.

Try a variety of leaves – flat-leaf parsley, rocket, sorrel, fresh oregano, sage or marjoram. Replace pricey pine nuts with walnuts, almonds or hazels. For oil, use a good quality sunflower or rapeseed. Add a dash of lemon juice or white wine vinegar. Be bold.

40

Two magic ingredients will

transform a Bolognese meat sauce.

The first is a dash of milk: add this to the base of onion, celery, carrot and meat and cook until absorbed. The second is nutmeg: add this after the milk but before the white wine and tomatoes.

41

Macaroni cheese

is now a 60s cliché. Here's a new – flour-free – version. Cook half a bag of penne or rigatoni and drain. Mix in ricotta or, better still, mascarpone, plus a spoon of mustard and some chopped soaked porcini. Add grated Parmesan and mozzarella. Seaon and bake in a hottish oven for 30 minutes

42

Couscous, invented in North Africa, **is the tiniest version of pasta.** It is also one of the simplest to cook. No boiling is needed. Put the couscous in a sieve and drench from the tap. Leave for 10 minutes, breaking up occasionally with a fork. Then steam it – if possible, over the dish it is accompanying – until tender.

43

Spaghetti alla puttanesca

– 'tart's spaghetti' – is racily named and irresistible. Cook 6 chopped anchovy fillets, 2 chopped garlic cloves and some chilli flakes in oil briefly. Add 2 tins of tomatoes, pitted olives and capers and cook for a few minutes longer. Toss with a bag of cooked spaghetti, plus some fresh parsley or oregano.

44

Gnocchi

just squeeze into the pasta category. Boil 1kg (2lb) of peeled floury potatoes and shove them through a food mill. Mix the potato with a beaten egg and 300g (10oz) of plain flour, kneading well. Cut into thumbnail-sized pieces and make a dent in each. Boil for just 10 to 20 seconds. Eat with butter and garlic.

45

Pasta and cauliflower

go together amazingly well. Divide the cauliflower into florets, boil and drain. Saute pine nuts, chopped onion and anchovies with soaked currants and saffron. Bung in the cauliflower and cook gently for 10 minutes. Mix with cooked bucatini and – the finishing touch – some breadcrumbs.

46

Many great pasta dishes call for very little cooking.

Try tagliatelle with tuna. Start boiling the pasta. Briefly saute a chopped garlic clove in oil, then add 2 tins of (drained) tuna, mashing with a fork. Turn off the heat and mix in some rocket and the juice and zest of one lemon. Drain the pasta and toss with the sauce.

47

Who wants yesterday's pasta?

Everyone, if you serve it up in a frittata. Heat the pasta gently in a frying pan with hot oil and garlic. Stir in chopped parsley and ham, plus grated Parmesan. Lastly, pour on 3 or 4 beaten eggs, making sure they are evenly distributed. After 3 minutes, finish off under the grill.

48

Leftover pasta will last a day or two

if stored properly. Mix it with a little oil to stop it sticking too much. Put in a plastic box or bag when cool, seal tightly and give a quick shake to separate. Keep in the fridge. To revive, put the pasta into a sieve and pour boiling water through it. Drain thoroughly.

49

Pasta salad should be made with care

to avoid that porridgey deli look. Try cheese, walnut and pasta for a change. Into the cooked (tubular) pasta mix cubed fontina, gorgonzola and another Italian blue cheese such as *Bel Paese*. Add sliced celery and chopped walnuts. Dress with walnut oil and black pepper.

50

For a new experience,

seek out pizzoccheri, or noodles made with buckwheat flour. This Alpine speciality has a nutty, crisp taste. Try it tossed with chopped spinach, boiled and sliced new potatoes and fontina cheese, flavoured with fresh sage and sprinkled with grated parmesan.

Andrew Langley

Andrew Langley is a knowledgeable food and drink writer. Among his formative influences he lists a season picking grapes in Bordeaux, several years of raising sheep and chickens in Wiltshire and two decades drinking his grandmother's tea. He has written books on a number of Scottish and Irish whisky distilleries and is the editor of the highly regarded anthology of the writings of the legendary Victorian chef Alexis Soyer.

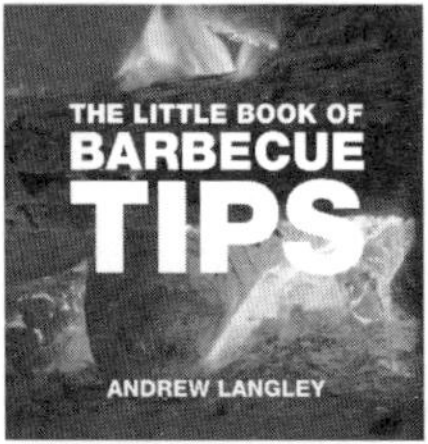
THE LITTLE BOOK OF
BARBECUE
TIPS
ANDREW LANGLEY

THE LITTLE BOOK OF
BEER
TIPS
ANDREW LANGLEY

THE LITTLE BOOK OF
HERB
TIPS
WILLIAM FORTT

THE LITTLE BOOK OF
POKER
TIPS
PETER FRENCH

THE LITTLE BOOK OF
GARDENING
TIPS
WILLIAM FORTT

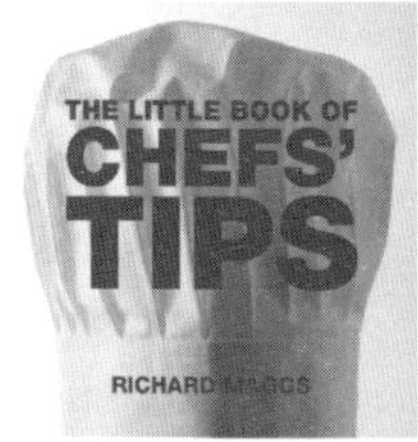
THE LITTLE BOOK OF
CHEFS'
TIPS
RICHARD

THE LITTLE BOOK OF
SPICE
TIPS
ANDREW LANGLEY

THE LITTLE BOOK OF
GOLF
TIPS
PETER FRENCH

THE LITTLE BOOK OF
TIPS
SERIES

THE LITTLE BOOK OF
CHEESE
TIPS
ANDREW LANGLEY

THE LITTLE BOOK OF
WINE
TIPS
ANDREW LANGLEY

THE LITTLE BOOK OF
AGA
TIPS 2
RICHARD MAGGS

THE LITTLE BOOK OF
COFFEE
TIPS
ANDREW LANGLEY

THE LITTLE BOOK OF
TEA
TIPS
ANDREW LANGLEY

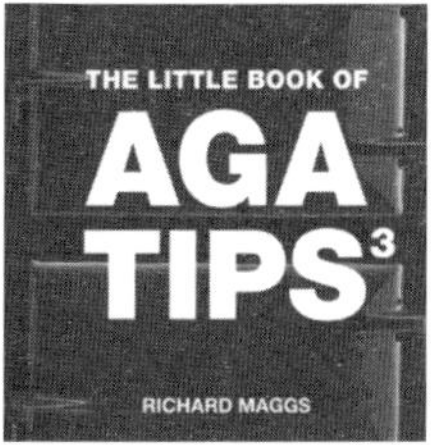
THE LITTLE BOOK OF
AGA
TIPS 3
RICHARD MAGGS

THE LITTLE BOOK OF
AGA
TIPS
RICHARD MAGGS

THE LITTLE BOOK OF
CHRISTMAS
AGA
TIPS
RICHARD MAGGS

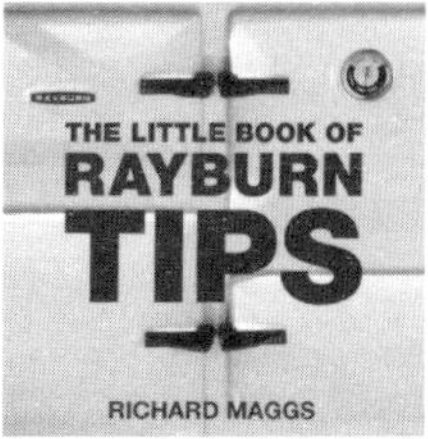
THE LITTLE BOOK OF
RAYBURN
TIPS
RICHARD MAGGS

THE LITTLE BOOK OF
BRIDGE
TIPS
PETER FRENCH
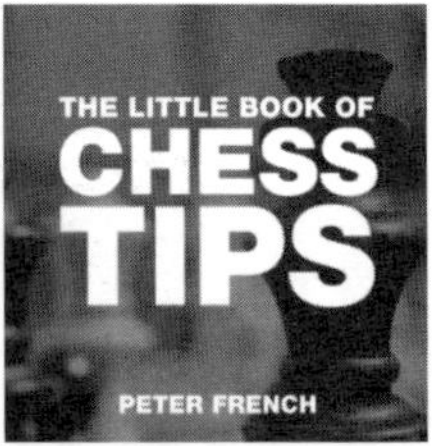
THE LITTLE BOOK OF
CHESS
TIPS
PETER FRENCH
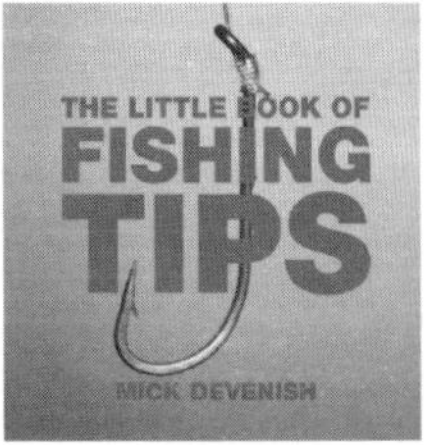
THE LITTLE BOOK OF
FISHING
TIPS
MICK DEVENISH

THE LITTLE BOOK OF
GREEN
TIPS
WILLIAM FORTT
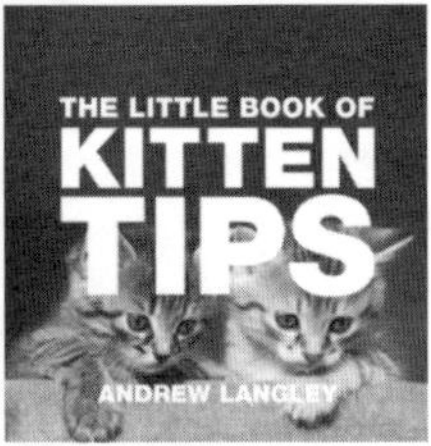
THE LITTLE BOOK OF
KITTEN
TIPS
ANDREW LANGLEY

MARMITE
PAUL HARTLEY
THE LITTLE BOOK OF
MARMITE
TIPS

THE LITTLE BOOK OF
PUPPY
TIPS
ANDREW LANGLEY

THE LITTLE BOOK OF
WHISKY
TIPS
ANDREW LANGLEY

THE LITTLE BOOK OF
TRAVEL
TIPS
MEGAN DEVENISH

Little Books of Tips from Absolute Press

Aga Tips
Aga Tips 2
Aga Tips 3
Christmas Aga Tips
Rayburn Tips
Tea Tips
Coffee Tips
Wine Tips
Whisky Tips
Beer Tips
Cocktail Tips
Cheese Tips
Bread Tips
Herb Tips
Spice Tips
Curry Tips
Marmite Tips
Olive Oil Tips
Vinegar Tips
Pasta Tips
Cupcake Tips
Cake Decorating Tips
Macaroon Tips
Chocolate Tips
Ice Cream Tips
Chefs' Tips
Barbecue Tips
Gardening Tips
Houseplant Tips
Golf Tips
Travel Tips
Fishing Tips
Green Tips
Frugal Tips
Poker Tips
Bridge Tips
Chess Tips
Backgammon Tips
Scrabble Tips
Puppy Tips
Kitten Tips